DARWIN'S TREE OF LIFE

Michael Bright ~ Margaux Carpentier

Crocodile Books, USA
An imprint of Interlink Publishing Group, Inc.
www.interlinkbooks.com

This edition first published in 2024 by
Crocodile Books
An imprint of Interlink Publishing Group, Inc.
46 Crosby Street, Northampton, MA 01060
www.interlinkbooks.com

Published simultaneously in the UK by Wayland

Managing Editor: Victoria Brooker
Designer: Anthony Hannant, Little Red Ant
Consultant: Michael Benton, Professor of Vertebrate Palaeontology and Head of School
of Biological Sciences, University of Bristol

Library of Congress Cataloging-in-Publication Data
Names: Bright, Michael, author. | Carpentier, Margaux, illustrator.
Title: Darwin's tree of life / written by Michael Bright ; illustrated by Margaux Carpentier.
Description: Northampton, MA : Crocodile Books, an imprint of Interlink Publishing
Group, Inc., 2019. | Audience: Ages 9-12. | Includes index.
Identifiers: LCCN 2019000273 | ISBN 9781623719197 (hardcover) |
ISBN 9781623717070 (paperback)
Subjects: LCSH: Evolution (Biology)—Juvenile literature.
Classification: LCC QH367.1 .B74 2019 | DDC 576.8—dc23
LC record available at https://lccn.loc.gov/2019000273

Printed and bound in China
10 9 8 7 6 5 4 3 2 1

MIX
Paper | Supporting
responsible forestry
FSC® C144853

Contents

The Tree of Life

Charles Darwin (1809–1882) traveled the world studying plants and animals. While in the Galápagos Islands, he collected birds called finches. The ornithologist John Gould (1804–1881) noticed that on each island the birds had differently shaped beaks. Had they evolved beaks that were best suited to the food available locally?

Observations like this led Darwin to propose his theory of evolution. He suggested that every species has evolved from earlier life forms. The first ones appeared billions of years ago, and they evolved gradually into the millions of species living on the Earth today.

CHARLES DARWIN

LIFE CHANGES

Evolution happens because baby plants and animals inherit most of their parents' features, but a few things might change. The changes might make the baby more likely to survive and pass that advantage on to its own young. Those without the difference might die out. Scientists call it "natural selection" or "survival of the fittest."

DARWIN'S "TREE OF LIFE"

Darwin wrote a book called *The Origin of Species* (1859) in which he compared the classification of living things to the branches of a tree. It shows the order in which plants and animals evolved, with the earliest living things on the lower branches. Branches close together show related groups. Where one group evolves into another, the branch divides.

MEET THE FAMILY

The Tree of Life is about relationships. You are closely related to your parents, and all the people in your family are related to grandparents, and then great-grandparents, and so on, back in time. Plants and animals are the same. However, if we trace our ancestors back to the very beginning, we find that our first ancestor was the same ancestor of every plant and animal on the planet. We all evolved from the same living thing billions of years ago.

The Dawn of Life

Life may have begun when a bolt of lightning zapped chemicals in a shallow pond, or in hot water vents deep in the sea. Nobody knows for sure. But the first living things were simple cells, which were different from non-living things because they could make copies of themselves.

ANCIENT THINGS

The first living things evolved about 4 billion years ago. They were similar to single-celled Archaea, the most ancient group of organisms on Earth today. Some live in extreme habitats. One unusual species forms flat sheets of square-shaped cells in saltwater lakes.

BACTERIA

ARCHAEA

CHANGING THE EARLY EARTH'S ATMOSPHERE

Bacteria are similar to Archaea: single cells without a nucleus. Some can make their own food using water, carbon dioxide, and energy from the Sun. This process is called photosynthesis, and oxygen is a waste product. It is thought that bacteria like this produced the first oxygen in Earth's atmosphere about 3.5 billion years ago.

CREATURES THAT ARE NOT PLANTS, ANIMALS, OR FUNGI

Protists are unrelated living things. Many consist of a single cell with a nucleus. The animal-like amoeba, the *Paramecium*, and the fungus-like slime molds are very different, but they are grouped together as protists, because nobody is sure how to classify them!

PARAMECIUM

TRICHOPLAX

THE WORLD'S LARGEST LIVING THING

The first fungi lived about 2.4 billion years ago deep beneath the ocean floor. Today, fungi come in all shapes and sizes, from single-cell yeasts to the largest living thing on Earth—a honey fungus whose filaments cover an area 2.4 miles (3.8 km) across! Fungi are more closely related to animals than plants, and cannot produce their own food.

THE BIRTH OF ANIMALS

About 700 million years ago, almost the entire planet froze over, a period known as "Snowball Earth." When the big thaw arrived, rock ground up by glaciers was washed into the sea. This natural fertilizer increased algae in the oceans, which became food for the first animals. These animals were made of many cells. Some were probably flat and shapeless, like the modern millimeter-long Trichoplax.

FLY AGARIC MUSHROOM

Early Land Plants

Scientists believe that green plants evolved from green algae. The algae lived in water, but some survived in damp places on land. Over millions of years, these algae gradually evolved into small, green plants. By about 450 million years ago, many new species had appeared, and spread across the world.

LIVER-LIKE SMALL PLANTS

Liverworts were among the first land plants—fossils have been found dated 473 million years old. Modern liverworts are anchored to the soil by root-like hairs, rather than proper roots, and are spread either by scattering spores or with little buds of tissue (gemmae) scattered by raindrops.

LIVERWORTS

LIVING CUSHIONS

Mosses joined the liverworts as pioneers on land, and together they changed the Earth's climate. The atmosphere had contained high levels of carbon dioxide (CO_2), which acted like glass in a greenhouse and kept the Earth warm. When the first plants appeared, they removed CO_2 during photosynthesis and the Earth's atmosphere cooled.

MOSSES

HORSETAILS

ANCIENT SWAMP FORESTS

About 350 million years ago, horsetails grew to 100 feet (30 m) tall and formed the swamp forests of the Carboniferous period, together with other tree-like plants. Their remains turned into coal. Nowadays, most horsetails are only about 6 feet (2 m) tall.

FERNS

GREEN FRONDS

Most of the ferns we know today appeared during the Cretaceous period. They were tough: after the asteroid impact that wiped out the dinosaurs 66 million years ago (see pages 20–21), the ferns survived. They covered most of the Earth's land surface for the next 100,000 years.

Seed Producers

By the beginning of the Carboniferous period, about
360 million years ago, land plants were developing
roots, leaves, wood, pollen, and seeds. The ancestors of
cycad and conifer trees grew tall during the drier Permian
period that followed, replacing the swamp forests.
However, it was not until the early Cretaceous period,
about 140 million years ago, that the first flowers bloomed.

CYCADS

BEETLE BENEFITS

Ancient palm-like trees called
cycads were widespread by the
mid-Permian period. Over millions
of years they have developed close
relationships with other living things to
help them survive. Each type of modern
cycad, for example, is pollinated by
its own species of beetle.

CONES

EVERGREEN FORESTS

Conifers, along with the cycads, were
food for plant-eating dinosaurs. These
trees produce cones, like the pine cone,
to protect and help spread their seeds.
Today, the world's tallest trees are conifers—
coast redwoods grow up to 378 feet (115 m) tall.

EARLY BLOOMS

Water lilies were among the earliest flowering plants.
The flowers of some species of water lilies attract insects,
and scientists believe the evolution of flowering plants
and insects is intertwined. Flowering plants rely on
insects for pollination and insects rely on flowers for food.

WATER LILIES

FOOD FOR THE WORLD

Grasses appeared during the Cretaceous period, and their remains
have been found in fossilized dinosaur dung. Today, they are the most
widespread group of plants, covering nearly half of the Earth's land
surface. About three-quarters of all the crops we grow are grasses.

WHEAT

BARLEY

RICE

MAIZE

COAST REDWOOD

11

Rise of the Animals

Over 600 million years ago, during the Ediacaran period, an extraordinary array of animals began to appear. Some were unlike any animals living today and some, like *Charnia*(E),* were more like plants than animals. Among them were the first signs of more familiar creatures: *Arkarua* (E) had a five-pointed star pattern, like a starfish.

*An (E) next to an animal means that it is now extinct.

CHARNIA (E)

ARKATUA (E)

SIMPLE ANIMALS

Sponges were among the earliest animals, and even today they are relatively simple. They have no nervous system or muscle. They are the only animals that, if broken down into individual cells, can put themselves back together again.

BARREL SPONGES

JELLIES WITH HAIR

Comb jellies have eight rows of tiny hairs, or cilia, along their bodies. The cilia move like oars, propelling them through the water. Many have a pair of long sticky tentacles, to trap food. They are an ancient group of animals, already in existence 600 million years ago.

COMB JELLY

SWIMMING JELLIES

The oldest ancestors of modern jellyfish also lived about 600 million years ago. They were among the first animals to have a nervous system and muscles, so, like the comb jellies, they could swim rather than simply drift in the sea or sit on the seabed.

LION'S MANE JELLYFISH

REEF BUILDERS

Tropical coral reefs are built by polyps. Algae living inside them make food and give corals their color. When conditions change, such as a sudden rise in sea temperature, the coral loses its algae, turns white, and eventually dies. These delicate animals have almost died out at each major change in the Earth's climate. Such a change, due to global warming, is going on right now.

STAGHORN CORALS

13

Flats, Tubes, and the Indestructibles

About 541 million years ago, during the Cambrian period, the major animal groups we know today suddenly appeared. Scientists call it the "Cambrian Explosion." Among the new animals were worms and worm-like creatures. Now, they include flatworms, earthworms, worms that swim with paddles, and "worms" with legs. The bootlace worm can be up to 180 feet (55 m) long and is the longest animal in the world today.

EARTHWORM

RAGWORM

CHRISTMAS TREE WORMS

LEFT AND RIGHT, FRONT AND BACK

The ancient ancestors of flatworms were among the first animals that had a left and right side. They also had a head end, which meant they moved in one direction. Because the head encountered objects in the flatworm's living space first, it is where sense organs and brains developed. This is why our brain is in our head and not elsewhere in our body.

FLATWORMS

ROUNDWORMS

THREAD-LIKE ANIMALS

Nematodes or roundworms are slender worms without segments. Today, they live almost everywhere on Earth. Over half of nematode species live inside living bodies, including our own, where they are parasites. They are probably the most numerous animals on the planet.

WORMS WITH LEGS

Today's velvet worm looks like a worm, but has legs like a caterpillar's. Its segmented body shows how an earthworm-like animal might have evolved into an insect-like one.

VELVET WORMS

WATER BEAR

WATER BEARS

Tardigrades, or water bears, are the toughest animals on Earth. Less than a millimeter long, they can survive nuclear radiation and the vacuum of outer space. They can recover from drying out almost completely, and can live for 30 years without eating.

15

Armored Animals

During the Cambrian Explosion, predators and prey evolved weapons and defenses in order to survive. This battle to outdo one another might have been why there were so many new animals, including arthropods like the fearsome predator *Anomalocaris* (E). One defense was a skeleton on the outside of the body, and many of today's water-dwelling arthropods, which include crabs, lobsters, and shrimps, have this tough "exoskeleton."

ANOMALOCARIS (E)

ANCIENT ARTHROPODS

Trilobites (E) were among the first arthropods. Some slithered over the seabed as predators, some as scavengers, and others swam and fed on plankton. Trilobites were successful for 270 million years, but they became extinct at the end of the Permian period.

TRILOBITES (E)

EARLIEST LIVING ANIMAL

Crustaceans, like crabs and lobsters, are also arthropods. Some of the earliest were the forerunners of modern tadpole shrimps. One species, *Triops cancriformis*, has hardly changed in 220 million years, making it the world's oldest known species of living animal.

TADPOLE SHRIMP

RUNNING SIDEWAYS

The types of crab we see today did not evolve until the Cretaceous period, when they had to develop robust defenses against their predators, bony fish. One adaptation was to run sideways so their large claws always faced the predator.

BLUE CRAB

HORSESHOE CRAB

LIVING FOSSILS

Horseshoe crabs resemble crustaceans, but, like the extinct trilobites, are distantly related to spiders and scorpions. Fossils of horseshoe crabs have been found in rocks 445 million years old, so scientists refer to modern horseshoe crabs as "living fossils."

TIME OF GREAT DYING

About 252 million years ago, huge volcanoes spewed molten lava, which hardened into thick layers. The eruptions released vast quantities of carbon dioxide and methane, and the climate warmed dramatically. Acid rain killed the forests, and soil washed into the sea, making it acidic. Ninety-six percent of plant and animal species were killed off. This was the Permian-Triassic extinction, the worst there has ever been.

Lots of Legs

The word arthropod means "jointed leg," and this group of animals has a lot of legs between them. Insects have six, spiders and scorpions have eight, crabs and lobsters have 10, centipedes have between 30 and 354, and millipedes have up to 750! Some land arthropods have a waxy layer in the exoskeleton that stops them from drying out. Other land arthropods have to live in damp places.

EARLY LAND PREDATORS

Centipedes were among the first predators on land. However, they were and still are restricted to living in damp places as they do not have the waxy waterpoof layer in their exoskeleton. Modern centipedes, such as the Giant Tiger Centipede, can be deadly. Their front legs are modified as fangs that inject venom to kill prey.

GIANT TIGER CENTIPEDE

FIRST FLYERS

The first insects to live on land were successful because they developed a waterproof body and eggs that didn't dry out. Insects were the first animals to fly, and modern dragonflies resemble these early creatures. Their wings do not fold back as later insect wings do. Today, three-quarters of all animal species are insects.

DRAGONFLY

18

SPINNING SILK

Spiders evolved the ability to produce silk, which is light but incredibly tough, as strong as high-grade steel. They probably used it first to line nests and make egg cases. Eventually, they wove webs to catch food.

Golden Garden Spider

Deathstalker Scorpion

STING IN THE TAIL

Scorpions are great survivors. When times are tough they shut down their body, and can exist on just one insect a year, yet spring into action immediately if prey passes by. They evolved a stinger on the end of the abdomen for attack and defense. The modern deathstalker from North Africa's deserts delivers some of the most powerful venom of any scorpion.

MONSTER CREEPY-CRAWLY

The millipede *Arthopleura* (E) was the largest-known land invertebrate, up to 7.5 feet (2.3 m) long and 20 inches (50 cm) wide. It could reach such a size because millipedes need a lot oxygen to grow big, and in the Carboniferous era oxygen levels were one-third greater than today. There also weren't many large predators around to eat them.

Arthopleura (E)
(Giant Millipede)

19

Animals with Shells

Mollusks were also part of the Cambrian Explosion. Many mollusks today have protective shells, either a single shell, like a whelk, or a double shell, like a mussel. A cuttlefish's shell is on the inside. Some mollusks have lost their shells altogether, such as octopuses. This enables them to squeeze into places that most other animals cannot go.

OCTOPUS

OYSTER

BETWEEN THE TIDES

Oysters are ancient mollusks with two shells. Many species spend a lot of time out of water, on the seashore, which means they are exposed to extreme temperature changes. During the 250 million years they have existed, they have evolved a special chemical that protects them against high temperatures.

HOUSE ON ITS BACK

Gastropod mollusks are second only to insects in the number of living animal species. The garden snail is a common gastropod. It has a spiral shell and walks on a slimy "foot." The shell protects it from predators, and the snail can hide inside it in dry weather so it will not dry out.

GARDEN SNAIL

WORLD'S LARGEST LIVING INVERTEBRATE

The giant squid is a cephalopod mollusk. Its shell is reduced to a "pen" inside its body, which acts like a backbone, and the mollusk foot has evolved into eight arms and two tentacles. The giant squid lives in the deep sea, where it grows up to 43 feet (13 m) long. Its eyes are the size of dinner plates, the largest in the animal kingdom.

FLOATING FOSSIL

The nautilus family has hardly changed for 500 million years. The nautilus's shell is a spiral of interconnecting chambers, which it empties or fills with water to rise or sink in the sea. It can squirt water to jet-propel itself in a burst of speed. It is a living relative of the extinct ammonites.

CHAMBERED NAUTILUS

IMPACT!

About 66 million years ago, an asteroid slammed into the Earth, killing three-quarters of the planet's plant and animal species. Dinosaurs, nautilus-like ammonites (E), marine reptiles such as plesiosaurs (E), as well as many other creatures, disappeared completely.

AMMONITE (E)

Spines and Feet

Echinoderms are animals with a body based on a five-point pattern. They can be star-shaped, like starfish, almost spherical, like sea urchins, or sausage-shaped, like sea cucumbers. They all move on tiny tube feet that work by water pressure. The group first appeared in the Cambrian period, although an Ediacaran period animal showing the star pattern (see page 12) could have been a starfish ancestor.

STARFISH

STARS IN THE SEA

Starfish evolved by the Ordovician period, about 450 million years ago. They generally had five arms, although some modern species have more— a giant Antarctic species has 50. Some species can shed an arm and grow a new one, and some can remake an entire starfish from just a single arm!

HEDGEHOGS IN THE OCEAN

Sea urchins have a hard "test," or shell, covered in sharp spines. The first fossils of sea urchins are 450 million years old, but about 252 million years ago they were nearly wiped out in a mass extinction event (see page 17).

BLACK SEA URCHINS

SEA PIGS

CUTE CUCUMBERS

Sea cucumbers can be long or round, but most still show the five-point pattern with five lines of tube feet. They have adapted to live at every level in the ocean, from the seashore to the sea floor. The sea pig is a cute sea cucumber that looks a bit like a pig.

DEEP-SEA LILIES

Sea lilies, or crinoids, are anchored to the seabed by a stalk. They were the world's most common animals 450 million years ago, and they still exist today in the deep sea. Their close relatives, the featherstars, can swim by wafting about their feathery arms.

SEA LILIES

First Animals with Backbones

The ancestors of fish and other vertebrates appeared during the Cambrian period. The first fish-like animals had no jaws, and instead of a backbone they had a stiff rod called a notochord. The first fish with jaws and a backbone appeared in the Ordovician period, and became common during the Devonian period, a time scientists describe as the "Age of Fishes."

EARLY JAWS

Shark-like fish were swimming the seas 440 million years ago, and modern shark families appeared 100 million years ago. Sharks have a bendy cartilage skeleton, but stiff, rudder-like fins. The largest predatory shark alive today is the great white. This giant is capable of high-speed bursts when ambushing prey.

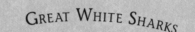
GREAT WHITE SHARKS

SWORDFISH

FASTEST SWIMMERS

Bony fish began to appear 420 million years ago. Modern fish have a stiff skeleton of bone, and bendy fins, so a few fish can actually swim backwards! The swordfish and sailfish are exceptional swimmers, the fastest in the sea.

"OLD FOURLEGS"

The coelacanth lives in deep sea caves in the Indian Ocean. Its ancestors were fish that evolved into amphibians, so the coelacanth is more closely related to amphibians, reptiles, and mammals than to swordfish or sharks, and its fins look a bit like legs. It was thought to have become extinct 66 million years ago, until one was caught in 1938 and nicknamed "Old Fourlegs."

COELACANTH

COLD-BLOODED

Most fish, amphibians, and reptiles have a body temperature that varies depending on their surroundings—they are "cold-blooded" or ectothermic. Many reptiles bask in the sun to warm their bodies so that they can be active.

Onto the Land

During the Devonian period, amphibians evolved from fish. Fish fins became legs and swim bladders became lungs. Today, many amphibians spend the early part of their life in water, first as eggs and then as larvae, such as tadpoles. Then they move onto land, but they still need to be in or near water to produce young.

TIKTAALIK (E)

FIRST FOOTSTEPS

Fossils of the amphibian-shaped fish *Tiktaalik* (E), which lived 375 million years ago, show how fish might have moved from water to land. Its fins had wrist bones, its eyes were on the top of its head, and it probably had lungs. Its fins may have supported the weight of its body, like a modern mudskipper.

WORLD'S LARGEST LIVING AMPHIBIAN

The Chinese giant salamander is a water-dwelling modern amphibian from a group that lived 170 million years ago. The group evolved into all modern salamanders. Most are less than 8 inches (20 cm) long, but giant salamanders are huge, up to 6 feet (1.8 m) long!

CHINESE GIANT SALAMANDER

GREAT JUMPERS

The ancestors of frogs and toads began to evolve during the Permian period. Many frogs can jump. The modern record-holder is the striped rocket frog, which can leap 6.5 feet (2 m), fifty times its body length. That's the same as a human long jumper leaping 330 feet (100 m) in one bound! It means these frogs can jump out of the way of danger.

STRIPED ROCKET FROG

AMPHIBIAN WORMS

During the course of evolution, the worm-shaped caecilians lost their limbs and burrowed in the soil. Here they were out of sight of predators. The modern mother caecilian has developed a unique way of feeding her offspring. Her babies eat the skin on her body!

CAECILIANS

Age of Reptiles

Reptiles had small, lizard-like beginnings in steamy Carboniferous swamps. They had a huge advantage over amphibians because reptile eggs could be laid on land. Eventually, during the Jurassic and Cretaceous periods, reptiles came to dominate the Earth. On land there were dinosaurs (E). In the oceans were ichthyosaurs (E), plesiosaurs (E), and mosasaurs (E). In the air there were pterosaurs (E).

TYRANNOSAURUS REX (E)

ICHTHYOSAUR (E)

BACK TO THE SEA

On land, there was such competition for food and living space that some reptiles returned to the sea. They looked like modern dolphins and sharks. The ichthyosaurs (E) gave birth to live young instead of laying eggs, a process that probably evolved on land.

SALTWATER CROCODILE

A DEADLY SMILE

Crocodiles shared the planet with the dinosaurs. They also shared the same ancestors, the archosaurs. But while dinosaurs walked with their legs directly below their bodies, crocodiles have their limbs splayed out on either side. At about 20 feet (6 m) long, the largest living crocodile is the saltwater crocodile, but the largest ever was twice as long and ate small dinosaurs for breakfast!

FAST-TRACK EVOLUTION

Lizards can evolve super-fast. In the 1970s, insect-eating wall lizards were introduced to an island in Croatia. They quickly adapted to a habitat with many plants but few insects. They evolved a gut to process plant material and a stronger bite to harvest it. Such changes would be expected to take millions of years, but these lizards made them in just 30 years.

ITALIAN WALL LIZARD

AFRICAN ROCK PYTHON

OPEN WIDE

Snakes evolved from ancient lizards about 130 million years ago. Modern snakes have more joints and stretchy ligaments in their skull than lizards and crocodiles. This enables them to open their mouths wider and swallow bigger prey. A large African rock python can swallow a small antelope whole.

GIANT TURTLES

The first sea turtle fossils date from 157 million years ago. The world's largest living turtle is the leatherback sea turtle. It's up to 6.5 feet (2 m) long, but its extinct Cretaceous relative, *Archelon* (E), was three times bigger.

LEATHERBACK SEA TURTLE

Living Dinosaurs

Birds evolved from meat-eating dinosaurs that stood upright on two legs. Some dinosaurs had feathers, which evolved from reptile scales. To become birds, dinosaurs shrank, and some of the smaller ones could fly or glide. Scientists believe that not all dinosaurs became extinct 66 million years ago, and that birds could be living dinosaurs.

BIRD OF PARADISE

OSTRICH

MOST COLORFUL SURVIVE

All birds are warm-blooded and have several different types of feathers, which enable birds to fly and keep warm. Feathers can also help to camouflage, or to stand out in colorful displays. Male birds of paradise have spectacular feathers to attract females. The female chooses the male with the brightest feathers.

FLIGHTLESS BIRD

The ostrich has wings, but is too heavy to fly. Instead, its wings keep it steady when running. By watching how it runs on two legs, scientists can see how dinosaurs such as *Tyrannosaurus rex* (E) might have moved millions of years ago.

WANDERING ALBATROSS

WIND RIDER

The wandering albatross is one of the world's largest flying birds. It has evolved long, narrow wings, like a glider. It can soar on the wind without having to flap its wings, so it uses little energy and can fly great distances in search of food.

BACK TO THE SEA

About 60 million years ago, penguins returned to the sea. Their wings evolved into flippers. The emperor penguin uses its flippers to "fly" underwater. It is the deepest diving bird, occasionally diving to depths of 1,845 feet (565 m). The deeper it dives, the fewer competitors it has for the fish and squid it catches.

INDIAN ROLLER

EMPEROR PENGUIN

Egg Layers and Pouches

Mammals evolved from reptiles during the late Triassic period, alongside the dinosaurs. Over many millions of years, cold-blooded, egg-laying, scaly reptiles became warm-blooded, hairy mammals. Today, most mammals give birth to "live" young, apart from the most ancient group of mammals, the monotremes, which still lay eggs. Unlike other mammals, marsupials carry their offspring in a pouch, instead of inside their bodies.

SEVERAL ANIMALS IN ONE

Monotremes—the platypuses and echidnas—are mammals that lay eggs, like reptiles, but they feed their young with milk, like other mammals. The echidna resembles a hedgehog, but the platypus is a very odd creature. It has a duck's bill, a beaver's tail, and otter's feet!

PLATYPUS

RED KANGAROO

BABY POUCHES

Baby marsupials are known as joeys. Marsupials nurture their joeys in the mother's special pouch. Joeys are born when they are the size of a peanut shell. They clamber into the pouch and attach to a nipple that gives them milk. A joey can grow quite large before it leaves the pouch.

SABRE TEETH

South America's sabre-toothed marsupial (E) was about the size of a modern jaguar and had canine teeth over 6 inches (15 cm) long. It hunted between 9 and 3 million years ago. It didn't have a strong bite, but, having brought down its prey, its large teeth were used to make deep bites to the underside of the neck.

SABRE-TOOTHED MARSUPIAL(E)

TASMANIAN DEVIL

KILLER JAWS!

The Tasmanian devil is the largest living meat-eating marsupial. It has powerful jaws strong enough to bite through bones. The animal is famous for its fierce, blood-curdling snarls and violent rages, which is why early settlers named it "the devil."

Big Babies

All female mammals have a placenta, which feeds the unborn baby in the mother's womb. The placenta only forms for a short time in marsupials, but is long-lived in "placental mammals," whose babies develop inside the womb for much longer. The earliest known ancestor of placental mammals is a 165-million-year-old shrew-like creature. Its closest living relatives are a collection of very different animals.

SLOW MOVERS

South America's sloths are no bigger than a small dog, but the extinct giant ground sloths (E) grew up to 20 feet (6 m) long and weighed 4.5 tons, as big as a modern elephant. They had long, curved claws to strip leaves from trees, and stood upright to reach high branches.

THREE-TOED SLOTHS

ELEPHANT RELATIVES

Dugongs, and their cousins the manatees, are the world's only plant-eating sea mammals. They evolved about 50 million years ago from land mammals, and their closest living relatives are elephants and hyraxes.

DUGONG

AFRICA'S ROCK RABBITS

Hyraxes are rabbit-sized, rodent-like plant eaters that live in rocky terrain in Africa. One extinct species was the size of a small horse. When larger plant eaters such as antelope and zebras evolved, they ousted the hyraxes from the best feeding sites, and hyraxes were pushed into the mountains. Their closest living relatives are elephants.

ROCK HYRAXES

WORLD'S LARGEST LIVING LAND MAMMALS

The three species of modern elephants—African bush, African forest, and Asian—are the survivors of a group that once included giant mammoths (E), mastodons (E), and dwarf elephants (E) no bigger than a pig. They all have, or had, a long, muscular trunk, which is used for breathing, touching, trumpeting, and even as a snorkel.

AFRICAN BUSH ELEPHANTS

WARM-BLOODED

Mammals are "warm-blooded" or endothermic—they generate their own heat. But some warm-blooded animals can lower their body temperature during the cold season or when food is scarce, and go into hibernation to reduce the amount of energy they use.

Bug Hunters

Insects and worms are abundant in nature, so several groups of mammals have special adaptations to help them find and feed on this rich supply of food. Insect-eating mammals, or insectivores, tend to have long, pointed snouts and sharp teeth, and a good sense of smell, but their eyes and ears are small. Many are "flat-footed" or plantigrade, a form of walking they share with humans.

TUNNEL DIGGERS

The mole is adapted to a life underground. It has large forelimbs built like spades for digging. It feeds mainly on invertebrates, especially earthworms, which it stores in an underground larder, up to 470 at a time.

EUROPEAN MOLES

ETRUSCAN SHREW

BIG APPETITE

The Etruscan shrew is the world's smallest mammal (by weight). Its small size makes it lose body heat rapidly, so it needs to eat up to twice its body weight every day to generate enough heat to stay alive. That's the equivalent of an adult human eating 1,000 quarter-pound hamburgers a day!

PRICKLY CUSTOMER

Hedgehogs have changed little for 15 million years. Their spines resemble porcupine and echidna quills, but none of these mammals are related. At different times in the past, each of these families independently came up with spines as a defense.

BLOOD MEAL

About 50 million years ago, bats became the fourth group of animals to fly, after insects, pterosaurs, and birds. They evolved from insect-eating, shrew-like mammals that could glide. While most small modern bats catch insects like their ancestors, vampire bats drink blood. They probably evolved from bats that ate blood-sucking insects from the skin of other animals.

37

VAMPIRE BATS

Running on Tiptoes

The ungulates are a varied group of mainly large land-living mammals that eat plants. They run on their toes, which are protected by hooves. The hoof consists of a hard, rubbery sole and a strong, thick nail wrapped around the tip of the toe. Horses and rhinos have an odd number of toes, while pigs, cattle, giraffes, and hippos have an even number.

PLAINS ZEBRAS

WILD HORSES

Horses evolved from animals no bigger than small dogs that lived in forests. As the climate changed and grass replaced trees, they could not hide from predators. Those that had longer legs and could run faster survived. Today, long-legged horses, zebras, and wild asses run on a single big toe on each foot—one toe causes less stress to a horse's leg bones than several toes.

LONG–DISTANCE RUNNER

The pronghorn is a mammal with long muscular legs that lives on the prairies of North America. It is the fastest animal on four legs over long distances. It is shaped like an African antelope, but is more closely related to the tall and gangly giraffe.

PRONGHORNS

HIPPOPOTAMUSES

WATER WAYS

The hippopotamus spends the day in water and comes on to the land to graze at night. Its head is shaped so that it can breathe, hear, smell, and see while mostly submerged. Hippos only live in Africa today, but before the last Ice Age (110,000 to 11,700 years ago), hippos lived as far north as the British Isles.

RETURN TO THE SEA

Whales and dolphins don't run and they don't have hooves, but they evolved about 52 million years ago from ancient land-dwelling, even-toed ungulates that did. Whales did not reach their enormous size until around 3 million years ago, when food became abundant only at certain times of year, so the bigger the whale's mouth, the better. The blue whale is the largest animal that has ever lived.

BLUE WHALE

Meat Eaters

Carnivores eat meat. They are expert hunters, each species with its own way of tracking, running down, and catching its food. Lion prides ambush and bring down large prey, such as African buffalo and wildebeest. Jaguars can crush a monkey's skull with their powerful jaws, and African wild dogs run down gazelles.

TIGER

STEALTH HUNTER

The tiger, like most cats, is a loner. It creeps up on its prey and pounces, using its powerful back legs, knocks the target over, and bites it in the neck. It then kills and eats it, hiding the leftovers for another day. Two million years ago tigers were smaller than those today because their prey was smaller.

GREY WOLVES

HUNTING TOGETHER

The wolf is a pack hunter. By working together, wolves can kill animals much bigger than themselves, such as moose. The wolf is the wild ancestor of the domestic dog, and dogs often show wolf-like behavior.

MIXED DIET

Bears evolved from raccoon-like ancestors about 38 million years ago. They are classified as carnivores, but several species eat other food when it is available, such as berries. However, most bears (including the bamboo-eating giant panda) eat meat when they can find it. Bears have switched from being strict carnivores to being general omnivores.

BROWN BEAR

ELEPHANT SEALS

DEEP DIVER

Seals, sea lions, and walruses probably evolved from otter-shaped ancestors that lived about 24 million years ago. The largest modern seal is the elephant seal. It dives to a maximum of 1.5 miles (2,388 m) deep to catch fish and squid, where it is safely out of the way of large predators, such as killer whales and great white sharks. It takes a nap on the way down and on the way up to save energy during the dive!

Mammals that Gnaw

Rodents form a large and varied group that includes rats, mice, squirrels, beavers, guinea pigs, and porcupines. Their front teeth keep on growing so they have to nibble constantly to keep them in check, but this also keeps them sharp. Many rodents live in large groups, such as in prairie dog cities and beaver lodges.

BROWN RATS

A SERIOUS PEST

The brown or sewer rat originated in northern China, but now lives wherever humans live, except Antarctica. This wily rodent eats just about anything, and its generalized diet has led partly to its success in conquering the world, much as we omnivorous humans have.

CAPYBARAS

GIANT RODENT

South America's capybara is a rodent that returned to the water and has slightly webbed feet. In the river, there is plenty of aquatic plant food. It is the largest living rodent, but the largest rodent that ever lived was the guinea pig-like giant pacarana (E), which was almost 10 feet (3 m) long and weighed a more than a ton.

HOPPING AROUND

Rabbits evolved from mammals that had shovel-shaped claws for digging. Over time, the longer hind limbs developed and the modern leaping gait evolved, enabling the rabbit and its cousin, the hare, to race away from its predators.

EUROPEAN RABBITS

TREE SHREW

PRIMATE PREDECESSORS

Tree shrews are small, slender animals with long tails. They have the largest brains compared to their body size of any mammal. They are not rodents or insectivores, but are related to primates, the group that includes humans. The ancient ancestors of primates were probably similar to tree shrews. They lived in the trees about 56 million years ago.

43

Skillful Mammals

Primates are animals with well-developed hands and feet. They are descended from tree-dwelling ancestors, and even today most primates live in trees. Today, there are two main groups, prosimians and simians. Lemurs, lorises, and tarsiers are prosimians and have more primitive features, such as a small brain. Simians—monkeys and apes—are more advanced, with a more complex brain than most other mammals.

AYE-AYE

ELONGATED FINGER

Wild lemurs live only on the island of Madagascar, off the coast of southern Africa. Before humans arrived on the island 2,000 years ago, there were lots of species, including one the size of a gorilla, but people killed them for food and many became extinct. Some lemurs are very unusual—the aye-aye has a strangely long, thin middle finger that it uses to prise grubs from rotting wood.

EXTRA HAND

There are two groups of monkeys: Old World monkeys in Africa and Asia, and New World monkeys in the Americas. New World monkeys probably evolved from African species that crossed the Atlantic via islands. The spider monkey is one of the few modern monkeys with a prehensile or grasping tail. The tail frees up the monkey's hands to hold the fruits, leaves, and flowers on which it feeds.

SPIDER MONKEY

PLANET OF THE APES

Gibbons, orangutans, gorillas, and chimpanzees are apes. They have large brains and no tail. Chimpanzees use tools to catch termites and make sponges from leaves to soak up water to drink. Male eastern lowland gorillas are the largest non-human apes, at more than 6 feet (1.94 m) tall. Chimps and bonobos (pygmy chimpanzees) are our nearest living relatives.

CHIMPANZEE

MODERN HUMAN

HOMO SAPIENS

Humans are apes with large and complex brains and lightly built bodies. We make complex tools, use fire to cook, build shelters, trade over long distances, possess spoken and written languages, create works of art, and study the world around us. Modern humans probably originated in Africa more than 315,000 years ago.

DARWIN DELIGHTED

The Tree of Life does not stop growing. New plants and animals are evolving all the time. The study of evolution is also evolving. New scientific techniques are revealing that evolution is not always a gradual process: it can happen quickly. Charles Darwin would be amazed and pleased to see new insights into his original theory of evolution.

Glossary

abdomen one section of an animal's body

absolute zero Negative 459.67 °F (-273.15 °C), when atoms stop moving

algae photosynthetic organisms, some with a single cell, such as diatoms, others with many cells, such as seaweed, but without true roots, stems or leaves

ancestor an earlier type of plant or animal from which more recent ones have evolved

aquatic living in water

asteroid a rocky space body, between 1 and 470 miles (1.6 and 775 km) across, that moves around the Sun

atmosphere the envelope of gases that surrounds the Earth and other planets

buoyancy the ability to float or move up and down in water

canines pair of pointed teeth that are next to the front teeth

cell the basic unit of a living thing that can copy itself independently of any other living thing

classification the arrangement of plants and animals into formal groups based on their similarities

climate change a change in global climate patterns either natural or human made

descendants plants or animals that have evolved from earlier ones

dominant having the power and influence over others

endangered close to becoming extinct

fertilizer chemical added to the soil or sea to make it more productive

filament thread-like structure

gene the part of a cell that controls the appearance and growth of a living thing. It is the fundamental unit of inheritance that passes from parent to offspring

global warming a rise in the temperature of Earth's atmosphere and oceans, either natural or human made

greenhouse gases gases in the atmosphere that trap heat like the glass in a greenhouse and keep the Earth warm. Carbon dioxide, methane, and water vapor are greenhouse gases

habitat the place where plants and animals normally live

herbivore an animal that eats plants

hibernation when an animal slows or shuts down its body and "sleeps" through periods of cold weather

incisors chisel-like front teeth

invertebrate animal without a backbone

ligament a band of tough tissue that holds together bones or cartilage

mass extinction when many plants and animals become extinct at the same time

nucleus the control center of a cell, where the instructions for its size, shape and function are held on genes (see "genes" above)

omnivore animal that eats both plants and animals

organism an individual plant, animal, fungus, protist, or bacterium

ornithologist a scientist who studies birds

parasite plant or animal that lives on or inside another plant or animal and causes it harm

photosynthesis the process by which green plants and other organisms manufacture sugars from carbon dioxide and water using the energy from the Sun. It generally involves the green pigment chlorophyll

plankton living things that drift in oceans or lakes

pollinate to carry pollen from one flower to another, which helps a plant make more plants

polyp the living part of coral, which resembles a tiny sea anemone

predator an animal that hunts and eats other animals

prehistoric very ancient, before the time of written records

prey an animal that is hunted and eaten by another animal

scavenger an animal that eats dead plants or animals

seagrass flowering plant that grows in the sea

sediments dust, sand, and other materials that settle on the land, or the seabed, lakebed, or riverbed, which in time form into rocks

species a group of similar individuals of plants or animals that can breed together. Their scientific name is written as two Latin words in italics, e.g. *Homo sapiens*

spore a tiny seed-like body that can give rise to a new fungus, moss, liverwort, or fern

tissues a collection of specialized cells in the body of a plant or animal, such as muscle or nerves

tropical living in a hot region of the Earth, located in a broad band on either side of the Equator

venom a poisonous substance produced by animals that is injected into prey or an attacker by biting or stinging

vertebrate animal with a backbone

waxy substance that repels water and can be used to waterproof something

womb the place in a mother mammal's body where her unborn baby develops

Index